Juggling Work and Home

The Toll on Motherhood

Pastor Jan Voerman

TEACH Services, Inc.
P U B L I S H I N G
www.TEACHServices.com • (800) 367-1844

World rights reserved. This book or any portion thereof may not be copied or reproduced in any form or manner whatever, except as provided by law, without the written permission of the publisher, except by a reviewer who may quote brief passages in a review.

The author assumes full responsibility for the accuracy and interpretation of the Ellen White quotations cited in this book. Unless otherwise indicated, all scripture quotations are taken from the King James Version of the Bible.

Unless otherwise indicated, all Scripture quoted in this book are from the King James Version.

Other scriptures are taken from *The Berean Bible* (www.Berean.Bible), *Berean Study Bible* (BSB) © 2016, 2018 by Bible Hub and Berean.Bible. Used by Permission. All Rights Reserved.

The Passion Translation® New Testament with Psalms, Proverbs, and Song of Songs is translated from Hebrew, Greek, and Aramaic texts by Dr. Brian Simmons.

The New Testament According to the Eastern Text, translated from original Aramaic sources by George M. Lamsa, Philadelphia: A. J. Holman Company, © 1933, public domain.

Copyright © 2019 Pastor Jan Voerman

Copyright © 2019 TEACH Services, Inc.

ISBN-13: 978-1-4796-1015-0 (Paperback)

ISBN-13: 978-1-4796-1016-7 (ePub)

Library of Congress Control Number: 2018961041

Scripture quotations marked The Message are taken from The Message. Copyright © 1993, 1994, 1995, 1996, 2000, 2001, 2002. Used by permission of NavPress Publishing Group.

Scripture quotations marked NASB are taken from the New American Standard Bible®, copyright © 1960, 1962, 1963, 1968, 1971, 1972, 1973, 1975, 1977, 1995 by The Lockman Foundation. Used by permission.

Scripture quotations marked NIV are taken from The Holy Bible, New International Version®, NIV®. Copyright © 1973, 1978, 1984, 2011 by Biblica, Inc.TM Used by permission. All rights reserved world wide.

Texts credited to NKJV are taken from the New King James Version®. Copyright © 1982 by Thomas Nelson, Inc. Used by permission. All rights reserved.

Scripture quotations marked NLT are taken from the Holy Bible, New Living Translation, copyright © 1996, 2004, 2007 by Tyndale House Foundation. Used by permission of Tyndale House Publishers, Inc., Carol Stream, Illinois 60188. All rights reserved.

Scripture quotations marked REB are taken from The Revised English Bible, copyright © Cambridge University Press and Oxford University Press 1989. All rights reserved.

TEACH Services, Inc.
P U B L I S H I N G
www.TEACHServices.com • (800) 367-1844

And these words, which I command thee this day, shall be in thine heart: And thou shalt teach them diligently unto thy children, and shalt talk of them when thou sittest in thine house, and when thou walkest by the way, and when thou liest down, and when thou risest up.

Deuteronomy 6:6, 7.

Juggling Work and Home: The Toll on Motherhood

Popular cries regularly heard in our days in the social sphere and sometimes in the church as well include:

- Men and women are created equal, without distinction.
- It is discriminatory to treat women in the workplace differently than men.
- Men and women should be able to perform the same functions.
- Women should work like men to build a social career.

Whenever one hears these clean-sounding slogans, it is important to ask: How do they work for women in practice, what exactly are their consequences, and what is the reality?

The commission that God gave to the first human couple is: "Be fruitful, and multiply ..."[1] As a general rule, it is God's intention that men and women form families and be blessed with children. With this thought in mind, we must ask: How can we fit these modern, good-sounding slogans into God's plan for humankind? Is it easy for a mother to build a career in society while

---
[1] Gen. 1:28.

fulfilling her duties in the family? Can the proper education of children effectively co-exist with a job in the labor market?

It is certainly not difficult to discover that working mothers usually have much to juggle and struggle with many problems. Many working mothers would affirm that this is so.

As an example, listen to the testimony of a working mother in the small country of the Netherlands. No doubt many other working mothers in other countries can identify with her experience as they cope with the same difficulties.

> Desirée, mother of Shae and a self-employed entrepreneur, says: ... I want 100% to be a good mom, 100% a good woman, 100% a good homemaker, and 100% dedicated to my business. As you can imagine, I just can't do that all properly. Sometimes I have the feeling that I really can't get anything completely done, and that makes me sad because I want it so badly ... I am someone who keeps on going, and I perceive that I am getting ahead of myself. For a very long time, I have not had time for myself, and I notice that I am really in the mood for it.[2]

Can God support careers for mothers if they cannot properly fulfill their motherly duties? Can God approve of mothers getting ahead of themselves and having no time for themselves? Does this ever fit into God's plan? Is it not clear that today's society is disrupted and not in balance with God's intention?

No one doubts that the life of a working mother is no bed of roses:

---

[2] "Werk en Moederschap. Hoe combineer je dat? 5 vrouwen vertellen..." [Work and Motherhood. How do you combine that? Five women tell ...], Available at http://1ref.us/pv, accessed 9/18/2018. Translated from Dutch.

"As a working parent, you never really rest," writes entrepreneur and consultant Daisy Dowling in the *Harvard Business Review*. "Your to-do list is never finished and just seems to get longer, so that a sense of control is sometimes hard to find." "You actually have two jobs," says Dowling, "your job at the office, where you have to invest a lot if you want to go to the top or want to stay there, as well as your job at home because bringing up children is not nothing. Many parents are therefore stressed, perpetually tired, and insecure."[3]

Most of us working parents are focused on simply getting through the day, which—let's be real—is daunting. Yet that very determination to hunker down and

---

[3] Romy Donk, "Zo krijg je als werkende ouder weer controle over je tijd: 4 technieken" [How to get control over your time as a working parent: four techniques], available at http://1ref.us/pw, accessed 9/18/2018. Translated from Dutch.

conquer today's task list makes working parenthood feel even more overwhelming and relentless. Your task list owns you, rather than the other way around. Over 18 years (or more) of working parenthood, constantly feeling "I have a million things to do today" will be pretty disempowering and exhausting.[4]

Is it not apparent that our contemporary society is out of step with God's purpose?

Children of working mothers who are left at a daycare center or with a babysitter frequently become upset when left. A young working mother named Rocky wrote:

> But you also have to take into account the babysitter who tries to appease a screaming child and does not succeed. They are tired of that at a certain point, and I do not want my child to get the reputation of being unmanageable or something.
>
> From birth, his stable, constant factor was only mommy … I want to try it with another babysitter, but, as I said, they do not count on such a drama scene, and I also do not like it when it goes like that.[5]

A young mother named Nadiachal talked about her baby crying a lot at daycare.

> I am going to start working again tomorrow, two days a week. My little girl then goes to the nursery. She has been a trial and has cried all day. She can cry and keep on crying, and, actually, I am the only one who can comfort her. Also, understandably, she did not want to drink anything when she is so upset. It really hurts me.[6]

---

[4] Daisy Wademan Dowling, "How Working Parents Can Feel Less Over whelmed and More in Control," *Harvard Business Review*, January 12, 2018, available at http://1ref.us/px, accessed 9/18/2018.

[5] Rocky2008, "Zo weinig (tijd) voor mezelf" [So little (time) for myself], Oct. 4, 2011, available at http://1ref.us/py, accessed 9/18/2018. Translated from Dutch.

[6] Nadiachal, "Baby huilt veel bij opvang" [Baby cries a lot at reception], http://1ref.us/pz, accessed 9/18/2018. Translated from Dutch.

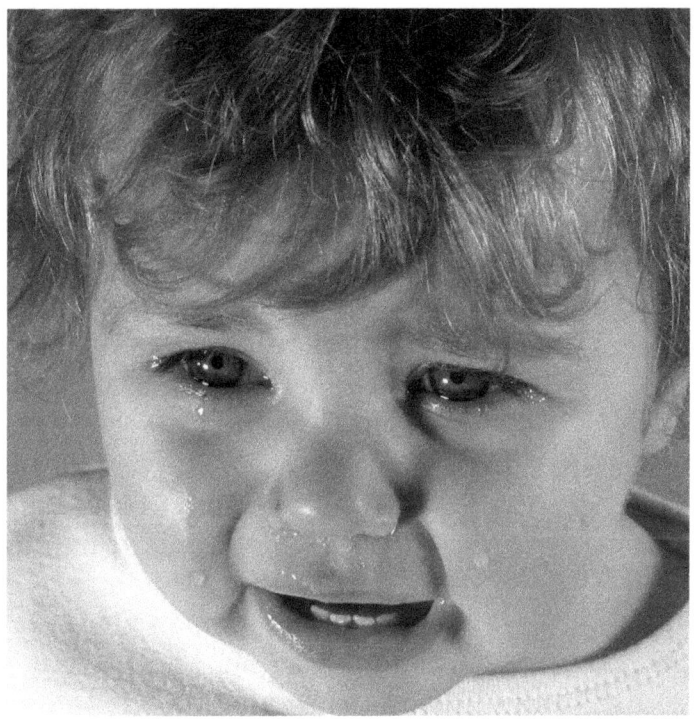

It is a fact that, when a child is very young, the tie with the mother is very strong and intense. Ellen White described the bond between mother and child:

> The tenderest earthly tie is that between the mother and her child. The child is more readily impressed by the life and example of the mother than by that of the father; for a stronger and more tender bond of union unites them. Mothers have a heavy responsibility. If I could impress upon them the work which they can do in molding the minds of their children I should be happy.[7]

The child that feels safe and secure with his or her mother is much calmer. The mother's presence is certainly beneficial for the sensitive child's soul, and it is necessary for the

---
[7] E. G. White, *Testimonies for the Church*, vol. 2, p. 536.

proper development and formation of an agreeable and balanced character.

Mother is everything, and, when a working mother places her young child in daycare, transferring the child's care to others, it is often with inconsolable crying. It is certainly no fun for the mother to have to go to work while leaving her child in tears. For the child, it is particularly a tragedy because the trauma leaves a big, often-irreparable fracture in the close and intimate relationship with his or her mother, which lingers for life in unwanted scars. The sensitive child feels that his or her mother is not there for him or her, and, even though the babysitter be sweet and patient and the caretakers be friendly, for most children, the mother cannot be replaced. Feelings of loneliness can creep into the fragile children's soul as they grow up, and they can become self-willed and self-centered. Does this sound a bit exaggerated? Remember, the first years of life are formative. They affect the whole life. Consider the warning of a specialist in this area: "Working moms are producing mentally ill children ..."[8]

The child that feels safe and secure with his or her mother is much calmer

Epidemic level of mental disorders

A leading psychotherapist has warned that mothers who return to work too soon after having babies are damaging their children's mental health.

"Our society tells women go back to work, do what you want, they'll be ok," she explained. "But they're not OK."

---

[8] Erica Komisar, "Working moms are producing mentally ill children, says author, *New York Post*, Feb. 27, 2018, available at http://1ref.us/q0, accessed 9/18/2018.

In a video for the *New York Post*, Erica Komisar revealed how she's seen an "epidemic level of mental disorders in very young children", which she puts down to the "devaluing of mothering in society".[9]

As a psychoanalyst and parent-guidance expert, I have seen society increasingly devalue mothering while idealizing work. At the same time, I have seen an epidemic of troubled children who are being diagnosed and medicated earlier and earlier with ADHD, early aggression and other behavioral and social disorders.

In my clinical practice over the past 20 years, I have seen again and again ways that these disorders connect to the absence of mothers on a daily basis in children's lives.[10]

Komisar wants working mothers to feel guilty so they will do as biology (allegedly) dictates and stay home with their infants.[11]

The author of *Being There, Why Prioritizing Motherhood in the First Three Years Matters* explained that babies experience a rush of cortisol and a great deal of stress when they're away from their mothers.[12]

Craving attention

She argued that when working women return from work in the evenings they spend as little as 90 minutes with their babies before they put them to bed—and then find that they don't sleep through the night as they're craving attention.

---

[9] "Psychotherapist warns that working mothers are producing mentally ill children – and claims the problem is at an 'epidemic level'," available at http://1ref.us/q1, accessed 9/18/2018.

[10] Erica Komisar, *New York Daily News*, May 14, 2017, "Just be there: Why moms should stay with children in their early years," available at http://1ref.us/q2, accessed 9/18/2018.

[11] Lauren Smith Brody, "New Moms Have Plenty to Deal With at Work. Don't Add More Guilt," available at http://1ref.us/q3, accessed 9/18/2018.

[12] "Psychotherapist warns that working mothers are producing mentally ill children – and claims the problem is at an 'epidemic level'," available at http://1ref.us/q1, accessed 9/18/2018.

"I started looking at the research which backed up what I was seeing in my practice, which is that the absence of mothers on a daily basis in children's lives was impacting their mental health."

Referencing research on attachment that's been done since the '60s, she said the only thing that reduces stress for babies is when their mothers return.[13]

Daycare, not a good option

"I still say daycare is my least favourite option," she said. "You're taking a very young baby and exposing them to a great deal of stimulation and a great deal of fear.

"When you take them out of their immediate environment and put them in a group with a lot of stimulation and a lot of people, that's not the natural environment for babies."

If you are away from your child during the day, Erica suggested two key strategies in the evening to try and offset some of the damage.

She said that all distractions should be "put in a basket," so that you don't look at phones, tablets or other gadgets while spending time with your child.[14]

The importance of the first three years

The psychotherapist said that motherhood must become more valued by society ...

"When we give mothers the option of being home in the first three years we increase the emotional security and reduce mental disorders."[15]

---

[13] "Psychotherapist warns that working mothers are producing mentally ill children – and claims the problem is at an 'epidemic level'," available at http://1ref.us/q1, accessed 9/18/2018.

[14] "Psychotherapist warns that working mothers are producing mentally ill children – and claims the problem is at an 'epidemic level'," available at http://1ref.us/q1, accessed 9/18/2018.

[15] "Psychotherapist warns that working mothers are producing mentally ill children – and claims the problem is at an 'epidemic level'," available at http://1ref.us/q1, accessed 9/18/2018.

Mothers serve two very important biological functions for children in the first three years. They soothe a child's distress in the moment, and they help regulate a child's emotions, not allowing them to go too high or too low. This lays down the foundation for resilience to stress going forward into adulthood.

When a mother or other primary caregiver is not present enough, a child experiences higher levels of stress. Research shows that when mothers and babies are separated, they both produce more cortisol, a stress hormone. The unrelieved production of cortisol may cause a baby or toddler to become anxious and fearful, even when there's no reason to be afraid. ADHD-like symptoms can be a response to stress in the environment, just as aggressive behavior can be a response to fear.

With parenting and young children, more is more. The more emotionally and physically a mother can be present for a child in the first three years, the better the chance that child will be emotionally healthy and mentally well.

Why the first three years? It is during this important time that mothers lay the foundation down for their child's ability to be resilient in the face of adversity throughout life and to be able to regulate their emotions

It is during this important time that mothers lay the foundation down for their child's ability to be resilient in the face of adversity throughout life and to be able to regulate their emotions going forward into adulthood

going forward into adulthood. By age 3, a child's right brain is 85% developed.[16]

The importance of maternal care

Fathers and mothers are both critical to children's development, but from a biological perspective, they are not interchangeable. In the first three years, it is particularly important for a baby's brain development that they receive more sensitive nurturing. A mother is more emotionally invested in her child, ... more committed to their safety and survival. Other caregivers, even fathers, do not have the same instincts.[17]

"On a societal level we need to recognise mothers work is valuable work. We emphasise material success and professional achievement, but there is no more valuable or more important work."[18]

Something is wrong, and the results are sure

Many of us have come to believe that our young children are "just fine" when we leave them for long stretches without their parents.

But something is wrong in this country. Too many young people grow up without the power to self-regulate their emotions. The U.S. Centers for Disease Control reports a 400% increase since the 1980s in children between the ages 12 and 19 on anti-depressants and anti-anxiety medications. Today, one in five children is diagnosed with ADHD.

These trends should have been no surprise. Research by Jay Belsky in the 1980s showed that children who spent

---

[16] Erica Komisar, "Just be there: Why moms should stay with children in their early years," available at http://1ref.us/q4, accessed 9/18/2018.
[17] Erica Komisar, "Just be there: Why moms should stay with children in their early years," available at http://1ref.us/q4, accessed 9/18/2018.
[18] "Psychotherapist warns that working mothers are producing mentally ill children – and claims the problem is at an 'epidemic level'," available at http://1ref.us/q1, accessed 9/18/2018.

more than 20 hours per week in childcare away from their primary caregiver before they were a year old were more aggressive and prone to behavioral problems in preschool. I've seen the evidence myself in my own practice.
In the distant past, cultures glorified the power of giving and nurturing life. Today, many women see themselves as warriors in the pursuit of power, money and work equality, and have turned away from nurturing as less than meaningful work. And yet they miss the point that mothering is the concrete emotional foundation of the house that withstands adversities and storms later in children's lives.[19]

More to gain than to lose

Yes, mothers experience sacrifices and losses when we prioritize our children, but there is more to gain in the emotional closeness and intimacy with our children than there is to lose. When my 6-foot-5, 17-year-old son hugs me and lays his head on my head and says, "Mom, thank you for always being there when I need you," it is all worth it.[20]

Many intelligent and driven millennial women are opting not to have children as they believe it's impossible to balance both family and career. With our present societal framework, they're right.[21]

"The truth is, we can do everything in life, but not at the same time. We cannot raise healthy children if we are not there for them emotionally and physically."[22]

Another source informs us

As many as 110 scientists, psychologists, doctors and other experts working in the United Kingdom want a

---

[19] Erica Komisar, "Just be there: Why moms should stay with children in their early years," available at http://1ref.us/q4, accessed 9/18/2018.
[20] Erica Komisar, "Just be there: Why moms should stay with children in their early years," available at http://1ref.us/q4, accessed 9/18/2018.
[21] Erica Komisar, LCSW @EricaKomisarCSW, 2018-04-06
[22] Erica Komisar, *Being There: Why Prioritizing Motherhood in the First Three Years Matters*, p. xi. http://1ref.us/q4, accessed 9/18/2018.

national debate as soon as possible on whether children under the age of three can be raised by others....

What researchers are increasingly concerned about is that high doses of the stress hormone cortisol are found in babies and toddlers in group daycare.

Psychologist and educator Steve Biddulph says: "The healthy development of the child's cerebral cortex depends on loving one-to-one care, but we have never had an economy or government that attaches so little importance to love".

"It is economically wise to give young parents more time for the upbringing of their children because it will prevent socially deformed young people from filling our schools, streets and workplaces.... What we need is quiet, caring people who can attach themselves and be close to them. We breed exactly the opposite."[23]

Young children in nurseries and daycare can count on serious problems in later life.

Note this report from the Scandinavian countries: Within the last 15–20 years, mental illness among girls has increased by about 1000 percent. Depression has increased by some 500 percent. The suicide rate of Swedish and Finnish girls is the highest in Europe; 39 percent of 24-year-old Finnish women have symptoms of depression. In young males, the trend is similar, if not so pronounced.[24]

Professor Dr. Manfred Spreng, a university professor in Erlangen, Germany, has been dealing with neurological and sensory physiology. He wrote more than 200 scientific articles in books and magazines about physiology—the

---

[23] "Natuurlijk Ouderschap [Natural Parenting] Attachment Parenting," available at http://1ref.us/qb, accessed 9/18/2018. Translated from Dutch.
[24] Anna Wahlgren, *Kleine Kinder brauchen uns* [Small children need us]. From the Swedish by Lore Rasmussen-Otten (Beltz Verlag, Weinheim, 2006), translated from German; Jan-Olaf Gustavsson, *Wie Kindertagesstätten eine Nation zerstören können* [How daycare can destroy a nation]. Human Life International; Info Nr. 4 (2001) und in Der Fels [and in The Rock] 2 (2002) S. 39-41.

science of the human body's function—in connection with hearing, language development, hearing in schools, the impact of noise, etc. In an article in the journal *Diakrisis* (April 2014), he investigates the causes of the high suicide rate among girls in Scandinavia. He points out:

> Especially alarming findings come from those countries that, like Sweden and Finland, have been portrayed as long-time role models for modern family politics and that—alongside Iceland and Norway—have been leading the way in Europe in gender mainstreaming for almost 30 years. In these countries, almost half of the 12-month-old infants and up to 90% (in Sweden) of the two-year-olds are entrusted to daycare centers (in Finland 97% of those under three years, in Denmark 78% of the one-to-two-year-olds). Interestingly, the female children and adolescents are especially affected.[25]

What does such care in nurseries or daycare centers do to the minds of young children, and what possible effects does the absence of a mother's care have on their development? Note Spreng's rather technical presentation of some alarming facts:

> The importance of acquiring close contact with the mother in the first three years of life and that of an undisturbed family environment cannot be overstated, considering the alarming analysis recently identified in the 2012 Barmer Medical Report. Based on large amounts of data, it has been found that 38% of boys and 30% of girls by age six have a speech disorder, which must be treated 20% and 14%, respectively, logopaedically [for speech defects]..... The Barmer Medical Report literally states: "These are disorders in which the normal patterns of language

---

[25] Manfred Spreng, *Diakrisis*, vol. 35 (No. 4) 2014, p. 9. Translated from German.

acquisition are impaired from the early stages of development."

Rather, there are phases of dedifferentiation (partial targeted degradation) and differentiation (targeted rebuilding) of the motor skills within the first years of life having points of time that are individually different and that can only be optimally coped with through continuous contact with the mother.

If the important structure and maintenance of the communicative relationship between mother and child is not sufficient or long enough, the infant's ability to imitate cannot be fully exploited, and apathy (learned helplessness) can result from failures in early childhood learning.

Circumscribed developmental disorders of speech and language often have secondary consequences, such as difficulties in reading and spelling, disturbances in the area of interpersonal relationships in emotional and behavioral areas.

The Barmer Medical Report conclusively points out that speech and language disorders usually start with an early onset of the disorder in childhood.

Looking at children as a whole in advancing genderism, one recognizes alarming tendencies. The gender image of gender mainstreaming ideologues, which is fixed on the employed woman, largely excludes the well-being of children and the interests of mothers who are at home....

Women are taught by almost all sides (especially by the business community) that it is a worthwhile goal to permanently reconcile family and work. This explains, in part, the strong political support of the possibility of gainful employment of mothers, which consequently calls for the care of children outside the home (nursery policy; nursery as state family compensation; in large cities there are now 24-hour daycare centers). It is therefore not surprising that the number of external care facilities already offered to very young children is steadily increasing (in 2008, it was approximately 14%; in 2010, it is already 23%).

General warnings are ignored or suppressed.... This is highlighted by the recent (2013) "National Investigation into Education, Care and Education in Early Childhood" (NUBBEK), funded by the Federal Ministry of Family Affairs. There it has been recognized that children from ages one to three would have been best kept at home if the social environment were right.

On the other hand, in these cases, which are relatively few in relation to the total population, care is better (optimal care ratio 1:2, i.e., one caregiver responsible for upbringing and no more than two children!), although the quality in more than half of the institutions must be described as inadequate.... But particularly problematic in the nursery are possible health problems and developmental disorders due to lack of sleep, such as stress hormone release and growth hormone reduction. Even in infants and toddlers, the diencephalon and the autonomic nervous system are fully functional, so that the loss of the solid attachment person—the mother—not only creates the feeling of abandonment, when the child is delivered to day care or the nursery, but an increase in stress hormone concentration (especially the substance cortisol) is also to be expected.

Indeed, it has been confirmed that, in infancy, being dropped off at the nursery and the departure of the mother may not only result in heartbreaking crying but, the traumatic separation and sense of abandonment will raise cortisol to astonishingly high and alarming levels. Numerous studies on children have substantiated these results....

Thus, it is a certainty that there will be worrying changes in the cortisol profile, in particular, when small children are cared for outside the family, even with high quality care. The toddlers' daily profiles of cortisol in nurseries are most similar to the stress reactions of managers who are exposed to extremely demanding professional expectations.

Cortisol, in contrast to the much faster reducing stress hormones adrenaline and norepinephrine, can cause a variety of problematic effects.

Interesting is the question of how an elevated cortisol level can adversely affect important maturation processes, especially in the brain of children. The region of the brain most affected by cortisol is called the hippocampus, which can also be simply referred to as the "learning machine of the brain."

Due to the influence of cortisol, shrinkage of the possible connections (the extensions of the brain cells, called dendrites) between the brain cells, with long-term death of the brain cells (called neurons) can be observed.

Thus, we should not only fear a negative effect on future stress regulation, but, through prolonged exposure to higher levels of cortisol in the infant through the damaged hippocampus collective, we are to expect adverse effects throughout the rest of the individual's life.

In addition, there is a risk of compromise in the prefrontal cortex (the forebrain area) and the amygdala (the amygdala of the diencephalon) next to the hippocampus. These are the regions of the brain that are responsible for both cognitive mental and emotional control. Other studies suggest that high levels of stress hormones, especially in girls, specifically affect this coordination, with the result that these girls subsequently have significantly greater anxiety management problems than girls who did not have high cortisol levels as children.

The more frequently a person experiences the deep sleep phase (or slow-wave) sleep, the greater is the production of growth hormone—especially for developing children. About 80% of adolescent growth hormone is only produced or released during this slow-wave sleep. An infant needs four to five hours more total sleep than an adult, and this greater number of hours of sleep during the day is partly in the crib to ensure appropriate phases of slow-wave sleep.... However, children who are less tired disturb other children, and among the cribs there is often an enormous noise level ... leading to disturbances in falling asleep and being able to stay asleep in the environment of the nursery, as well as delays in falling asleep.

As a result, reduced production of growth hormone is expected, with serious consequences for physical development and maturation of the brain, since the growth hormones are also involved in the growth and connection of nerve cells. Furthermore, it also thwarts additional stabilization of insulin sensitivity (the sensitivity of the blood glucose sensors) and glucose tolerance (the control of blood sugar levels), which increases the risk of diabetes and unnecessary weight gain (fat).... In fact, in a Canadian study, the proportion of obese children and children with obesity was found to be fifty percent higher in the former nursery and daycare children than among the children cared for in the family....

Far-reaching psychological consequences of the tendency to use external care services, which is largely triggered by gender mainstreaming, are clearly recognizable....

As reported, the apparent inability to manage stress and signs of anxiety, as well as depression and pronounced hyperactivity (ADHD = attention deficit hyperactivity syndrome) are startling....

A permanently high cortisol level correlates highly with a reduced size of the hippocampus. For example, a recent study found a correlation between attachment anxiety in later life and reduced cell density in the hippocampus of otherwise healthy young adults.... With further intensification of gender mainstreaming, one must reckon with the fact that not only are women, whose identity is questioned, increasingly depressed, but they can also expect impairments in physical health and the development of mental cognition and language. In addition, harmful influences from early and extensive outside care on an entire generation of children will have consequences for society as a whole, even if very few negative influences affect a large number of children.[26]

In the book *Child Guidance*, we read important passages that are clearly supported by contemporary science:

> Mothers, be sure that you properly discipline your children during the first three years of their lives.... Mothers should understand the importance attaching to this period. It is then that the foundation is laid.... The impressions made on the heart early in life are seen in after years. They may be buried, but they will seldom be obliterated.[27]
>
> The mother must ever stand pre-eminent in this work of training the children; while grave and important duties rest upon the father, the mother, by almost constant association with her children, especially during their tender years, must always be their special instructor and companion.[28]

Unfortunately, these words are hardly put into practice today. The many problems of the past are not getting better but only worse.

In addition to the harmful effects of separation on the children, consequences for the mothers are also great. Note this characteristic and candid testimony of a working mother who has tried, with great difficulty, to combine her family tasks with her job out in society. In

---

[26] Manfred Spreng, "Erlangen" in *Diakrisis*, vol. 35 (No. 4) 2014, pp. 4–10; cf. Manfred Spreng, "Kinder – Die Gefährdung ihrer normalen (Gehirn-) Entwicklung durch Gender Mainstreaming" ["Children—the threat to their normal (brain) development from gender mainstreaming"] in Andreas Späth and Manfred Spreng, *Vergewaltigung der menschlichen Identität: Über die Irrtümer der Gender-Ideologie* [Rape of Human Identity: About the Errors of Gender Ideology] (Ansbach: Verlag Logos Editions, 2015), p. 6; Manfred Spreng, *Es trifft Frauen und Kinder zuerst.: Wie der Genderismus krank machen kann!* [It hits women and children first. How genderism can make you sick!] (Ansbach: Verlag Logos Editions, 2015). Translated from German.
[27] E. G. White, *Child Guidance*, p. 194.
[28] E. G. White, *Child Guidance*, p. 24.

her post, "How I wrestle daily with the balance between work and motherhood," Janneke wrote:

> Despite my university degree, I did wish for a mamma day—a lot of mamma days. It just seemed fun to spend a lot of time with the children as long as they were young. Had I given birth to them to see them only in the evenings and on the weekend? So I cut back three of my working days, and the amount of work did not really decrease. Neither did the household chores. They only increased once there were children. And so I sometimes feel like a full-time manager of a complex business that consists of a full-time real job, besides a full-time job of caring, housekeeping, administration, playing, crafts, cooking, and so on. I keep so many balls in the air that I sometimes lose sight of a few of them. I forget a doctor's appointment or forget to email a customer back. I can't even think about having time left over for social life or anything like hobbies or the gym. It is a good thing that I like my work so much, otherwise I would have burned out from running the whole show.[29]

Is it really God's intention that a mother live constantly under tension and stress to properly balance her home and job? Looking for good solutions, it is not easy for Janneke to juggle all her tasks.

> It would help if we women were better at letting go—letting things go, as men often do so well. I find the latter a tricky thing. Before I had children, I let the house explode in such a way that the man of the house managed the vacuum cleaner. But now that I

---

[29] Janneke Jonkman, "Hoe Ik Dagelijks Worstel met de Balans Tussen Moederschap en Werk" [How I Worry Daily with the Balance between Maternity and Work], available at http://1ref.us/q5 (01-23-2018), accessed 9/18/2018. Translated from Dutch.

have children, I cannot do that anymore. I have tried it sometimes, but the children provide so much extra chaos that I just do not function anymore if the kitchen has also exploded. I suddenly lose important things such as house keys and the children's toys, and, what goes on in my head is just as chaotic as in my house. Moreover, I also work from that same house. My friend pulls the door behind him in the morning and goes to work elsewhere in the city on a tidy desk. If I let things go, then I look out on piles of laundry and dirty dishes throughout the workday. I cannot really concentrate, so to speak.[30]

Is it acceptable to God for a mother, rather than properly fulfilling her duties, to let things go more and more and feel unsatisfied while trying to make the best of it?

There is no question that Janneke has a hard time performing all her tasks properly, and it seems that she is sometimes at her wit's end. Yet, she is not alone. In a subsequent posting, on January 23, 2018, she added: "A great many women just can't cope with it anymore."[31]

In an article entitled, "Why Papa Is Relaxed and Mama is Unhappy," Vala van den Boomen wrote:

> Are you happy? Really happy? Are you satisfied with your life and how it is going? Many mothers are not, as evidenced in the research. Fathers, however, are having a good time. How is that possible?
>
> In my circle of acquaintances, I now have a lot of families with children. And what I see around me are fatigued mothers—tired, stressed, and grumpy mothers, mothers who are busy all day, keeping everything running....
>
> Renske recently wrote about this—that she had lost her groove. For years, she has been looking for

---
[30] http://1ref.us/q5 (01-23-2018).
[31] http://1ref.us/q5 (01-23-2018).

balance and cannot find it. I recognize the same, and I am sure that many mothers do too. I often feel that I have lost myself completely since becoming a mother. I feel that my own wishes and needs have completely disappeared into the background. And, at the same time, I feel that I am a failure if I do not continue to satisfy my own wishes and needs. We are supposed to be good, dedicated mothers, to be mindful of the education of our children, to have a career, to maintain a social life, and also to be a nice, attractive partner for our loved one. That's all fine and good, but can you tell me how?

There is a lot of criticism of mothers nowadays, that they complain too much…. But, should not we ask ourselves how it happens to be that so many mothers experience life as heavy and that there are so many mothers with burnout at home? I can see them collapsing around me, while each and every one of them are really strong women who are no pushovers. I feel it myself. So far I haven't collapsed, and hopefully won't do so soon, partly because I am blessed to have a man who shares proportionately in the care tasks, but sometimes I really wonder when there will be enough air for me to breathe again and my life will once again feel like mine. I think "unhappy" is a big word, but that many women feel that way, I do not really think so strange. You can leave the faucet running, but, at some point, the buckets will overflow.

So what to do to make the mothers of today happier? Whoever knows should tell us. I really do not know myself.[32]

---

[32] Vala van den Boomen, "Waarom Papa Relaxed Is en Mama Ongelukkig" [Why Papa Is Relaxed and Mama Is Unhappy], available at http://1ref.us/q6 (02-24-2017), accessed 9/18/2018. Translated from Dutch.

It is a well-established fact that working mothers, with their busy schedule of work and care giving, are less happy and more tired and stressed than men.

A team of researchers from Cornell University, the University of Minnesota, and Minnesota Population Center have used time diary data to find that mothers are less happy than fathers with their parenting duties. Mothers report more stress and greater fatigue than fathers.[33]

Motherhood has remained more or less out of sight for a long time, and it has been underestimated. Nonetheless, a recent survey has shown that motherhood can be compared to no less than 2.5 full-time jobs. That is certainly very impressive and absolutely not something to pass by unnoticed. It is, therefore, no wonder that many mothers are often stressed, tired, and unhappy when they also combine this heavy responsibility with a full-time job in the labor market. Is that not asking too much of the strength, vitality, endurance, and health of the human body?

Being a mum is the equivalent of 2.5 FULL-TIME jobs, according to new research

We've often heard the saying "being a mum is a full-time job"; but, according to research, it's actually closer to being two-and-a-half full-time jobs!

A new American study has found that the average mum works an astonishing 98 hours per week—over twice the average working week of 39 hours.

Researchers examined the schedules of 2000 working mums, with children aged five to 12. They found that the average work day of a mum starts at 6.23am and ends at 8.31pm.

---

[33] "All work and no play with children make moms less happy parents," available at http://1ref.us/q7, accessed 9/18/2018.

They found that even on their "free time", mums tended to fill their time with tasks; and, of course, the weekends were just as busy as the week days!

Most mums reported having just one hour and seven minutes of "me time" daily. We spend most of our "me time" in the bathroom trying to get a quick shower unaccompanied....

A recent survey has shown that motherhood can be compared to no less than 2.5 full-time jobs

Forty percent of mums surveyed said their lives felt like a series of never-ending tasks, while 70 percent reported feeling pressure to provide a healthy diet for their children.

"The results of the survey highlight just how demanding the role of mum can be and the non-stop barrage of tasks it consists of," said Casey Lewis, Health and Nutrition Lead at Welch's, the juice company that commissioned the survey, told *Yahoo*.

The survey also examined what "life-savers" mums relied upon when trying to do it all became too tough.

The extensive list includes wine (us too), grandparents or a reliable babysitter to step in from time to time, Netflix (for the kids or the parents), wet wipes, drive-through meals, healthy snacks and juices, toys and iPads.

Coffee, napping when possible, and the ability to put on an "angry" voice as required were also on the list of top 20 mum-approved lifesavers.

We can definitely testify to the power of all of the above in a stressful situation—particularly coffee in the mornings, or a glass of wine after a very long day.[34]

To achieve success in the labor market of today, in addition to their responsibilities within their families, women and mothers pay a heavy price, and their sacrifice is not always properly valued or acknowledged.

Also, the mothers who pretend to have everything well arranged are not stress and worry-free. They have their problems and longings just like everyone else. Often motherly pride plays a role. She creates a better image of herself because she is unwilling to admit that things have gotten unmanageable, and she has had to settle for less.

Mothers know from experience that the combination of a job and the duties of motherhood is difficult to balance, and it certainly will not perfectly be achieved without all kinds of cracks and dents. The toll on motherhood when it is combined with a job is huge in many ways, and its consequences are far-reaching.

Is it in harmony with God's will for a mother to always be in a hurry and chronically exhausted, often feeling dissatisfied because she has virtually no time for her-

---

[34] "Being a mum is the equivalent of 2.5 FULL-TIME jobs, according to new research," available at http://1ref.us/q8, accessed 9/18/2018.

self and always has to leave things behind since she is not an octopus? It is absolutely inconceivable that God would expect this of mothers.

Another question that is at least as important and urgent is whether God is concerned whether parents are meeting their responsibilities when they outsource the care of their affectionate, sensitive little children to daycare workers during the week because they are left with no time for their offspring, due to both parents' working full-time and building their careers.

> *Mothers know from experience that the combination of a job and the duties of motherhood is difficult to balance*

Consider the sad story of Brigitte, as described in the Dutch newspaper *De Telegraaf* on December 2, 1995. Important catchwords in the story are: *working parents, loneliness, no happy family,* and *divorce.* These are words that we frequently encounter in our disrupted society.

Brigitte is a heroin addict. She says that she does not use drugs for fun but to suppress her feelings. Which feelings are these? She explains that she always felt very lonely because her parents worked and she was an only child. Her parents had little time for her and for each other. What was not a happy home or a happy family finally ended in divorce.

Brigitte was fortunate to have a horse that she loved and through which she sought comfort, but, as a result of the divorce, the horse had to be sold and she had to give up that which she held dear. Brigitte left home, and her unhappy later life ended up wasted at the edges of society. Fortunately, fate is not always so dramatic, but there is an important lesson in her experience. Was it really wise for both of her parents to work to pursue economic security and independence?

What did Brigitte's parents win? In cases like this, even though we seem to be successful with everything we have gained, we will eventually have to admit before God's throne that we have *lost* everything that is important.

It is of eternal value for us to seriously consider our course of life and our actions and ask: Is it worth it for the father and the mother to both work and have less time and attention for their children to raise them up in faith to God's honor and glory? We should not underestimate the value of time and thought for our children. Optimistically we can view things as not being too bad and believe that, with proper counsel and planning, we can keep up with the responsibilities of the home while participating in the workforce. However, in practice, we inevitably run into all sorts of difficulties and problems in balancing the two!

An Internet site gives us a general impression of a mother's daily program blending home and work. Some stress points and tips are listed:

The combination of work and a family is heavier than you thought.

Having a job in addition to taking care of one or more children is no easy task. In both areas, you want to give 100%, and that is practically impossible. This is also called "combination stress." What can a person do to ease that pressure a bit?

Combine work and family

Combining work and a family is not an easy task. You may have thought it out properly in advance, but, in practice, it is often disappointing. Many parents experience it and compare it to keeping many balls in the air or to a house of cards—the balance is so delicate that it only takes something small to disrupt the entire balance. You also have to deal with many different stress factors.

Morning rush hour

Before you can leave the house, a lot has to happen. In addition to your own morning ritual and that of your partner, your child also needs to be dressed and fed. That takes time. In addition, when your child becomes a bit older, your child may well linger in the morning. He does not really understand the usefulness of being on time in daycare or at school. Playing is much more fun. So some of your educational skills are also requested at that moment.

You travel a little before you are at work

Usually you take your child to an outside childcare when you start working. Thus, that requires an extra ride before you can start for your work destination. Do you suffer from traffic jams? Then you can feel that you have to race against the clock every day.

Get away from work in time

We assume that you can spend your workday normally. You may be a bit mentally absent because of (more or less chronic) sleep deprivation, but, in principle, you have your hands free all day to spend on your work. By the end of the day, it will be a little more stressful: you really want to finish something, but you have to leave in time to pick up your child.

Evening rush hour

And then the same rush hour begins as this morning, but this time in reverse. From work, you drive past the daycare center to your home. There you will cook, eat, and put your child to bed. Usually, after everything, you will exhaustedly sit down to the side at half past nine. Now you have the time to yourself. Do you still exercise or go out? Or do you prefer to be away from crowds while you watch television?

All other things come in last place

Your days are filled quickly when you work as a parent. And we have not even mentioned all the additional jobs you have to deal with: shopping, paying insurance, buying birthday gifts, having a broken central heating boiler repaired, or driving the car for maintenance to the garage. So, that is all in your spare time, which is always so scarce.

You do only a little bit of housework

In addition to working and caring for your child, keeping a household going is quite a challenge. You often see with sadness the ever-growing stacks of laundry and toys lying around. It means fighting against the bar.

Your child is ill: what now?

As we have said, the balancing act is a delicate one. Because everything functions and connects, it does not allow for anything else to go wrong. If your child becomes ill, then you have to make a change. Which of you can stay home? Who has the least urgent appointments? Can you ask someone to look after your child? In the end, you may always find a solution. But the moment you realize that your child cannot go to daycare or school can cause a lot of stress.

Pregnancy and stress

Do you also think about expanding your family in the midst of all the bustle? Try to reduce stress in time because persistent stress is not good for the development of your unborn child.

What can you do?

All in all, the combination of work and child-rearing can be quite stressful. Here are a few tips to reduce the pressure.

Make good arrangements with your partner

Women often tend to attract more of the jobs in the home. Stop that. Create an honest and clear division of tasks between you and your partner, and stick to it. Do what you have to do and no more. Check regularly to see whether you need to adjust your appointments.

Buy as much as possible

You can outsource many practical jobs. Don't forget that fact, and do it! In actuality, you will buy extra time and rest. Make use of everything that can be of help in combining work and the care of the family.

Do not set the bar too high

Accept that you have a busy existence and do not try to reach the highest possible level on all fronts. Every once in a while, eat soup and sandwiches in the evening, or let your child go to school in a worn pair of pants. How important is that really? Good enough is good enough!

Use the legal rights that you have as a parent

You are entitled to a number of types of family leaves if you have or will be having children. Also, use that resource.

Get up earlier

There are parents who swear by getting up early. It is so good to have the first half hour for yourself at home to have a quiet shower, prepare sandwiches, or read the newspaper on the Internet. See for yourself if you do not find it worthwhile to give up some sleep for it.[35]

No doubt, having a perfect combination of work and home life for the mother is simply not possible. You simply cannot do everything at once. It undisputedly creates many worries and problems, causing the mother to sacrifice on many fronts and to settle for less.

What does society have to offer mothers in their workload?

Well, it all comes down to mothers' learning to accommodate themselves as much as possible to their lot in joining the treadmill of today's society of work and home, employing others to look after their children because there is apparently no way back from the gains that women have made in the workplace. It is considered a great good for mothers to help build the economy through their efforts in the labor market. Society's motto is: "Working mothers with childcare!"

The Dutch Government is satisfied with the current trend. Lodewijk Asscher, Minister of Social Affairs and Employment said:

> It is fantastic to see that more and more mothers work and that their children can turn to good quality and affordable care.
>
> In the second quarter of 2017, 293,000 children went to daycare, 341,000 to out-of-school care and 121,000 children to childminders. Some children use multiple forms of care.[36]

---

[35] Marèse Peters, "De combinatie van werken en een gezin is zwaarder dan je dacht" [The combination of work and a family is heavier than you thought], available at http://1ref.us/q9, accessed 9/18/2018.

[36] Renske Baars, "Kinderopvang steeds populairder onder werkende ouders" [Child care increasingly popular among working parents], available at http://1ref.us/qa, accessed 9/18/2018. Translated from Dutch.

These figures for a small country like the Netherlands are identical to those of other countries and are perhaps even worse, since we must ask ourselves: Is it really so wonderful for mothers to work and take their children to daycare?

The results on the family and societal levels for working mothers have not been so wonderful for many years.

Richard Whitfield, a prominent British scholar, writer, social scientist, and chairman of the National Family Trust, raised a red flag many years ago, writing in the British International Newspaper *The Guardian*, September 1991, that there is a major crisis in parents' care of their children, an alarming deterioration of unconditional love. He interviewed several school principals who told him that the children with problems usually are those who have not gotten enough attention because both of their parents work. These children often feel lonely, are rebellious, and show antisocial and disorderly behavior.

In the TV program of Cees Grimbergen, titled "Vesuvius, I or my child," televised by IKON (Interchurch Broadcast Netherlands), on the television station NL 1 on January 18, 1996, several people shared their parenting problems. Professor Doctor Trudie Knijn, chief of staff of social sciences at the University of Utrecht, explained that, for mothers, the consequences of full-time work are often disastrous. There is a major crisis in the education of their children, due to a lack of proper parenting. Many serious problems, such as criminality among young people, have greatly increased. Children are not properly cared for. They do not receive the quality of love they need so badly because both parents work and are too busy.

Do you disagree with this analysis, believing that this is not always the case and that there are many examples of things going well? Do you view this book as having been written in an excessively negative way? If you support women's ordination to the ministry, that could certainly be your opinion. But remember, sticking your head in the sand is not helpful, for there is certainly sufficient well-founded and candid information available to substantiate the premise of this book.

The hard facts do not lie. Our society is clearly undergoing disruption. There are many derailed children; there is a clear increase in youth criminality. Divorces, intolerance, burnout, chronic fatigue, quarrelling, lovelessness, disobedience, a lack of proper norms and values, selfishness, self-indulgence, obstinacy, rebellion and other bad manners are now, more than ever, the hallmark of the times in which we live.

> *The hard facts do not lie. Our society is clearly undergoing disruption*

But what can be expected when children are outsourced and their working parents do not give them the attention and love they deserve? When they do not receive steady input from their parents and they grow up and become more independent, the problems in inappropriate behavior and untoward excess that we have to cope with will become obvious! Having two working parents definitely has a negative side to it. No wonder professionals in the field talk about a major crisis in parenting and child rearing. No wonder the consequences for full-time working moms have so often been disastrous. The present situation is not what God intended. Yet, it is an inevitable result if we follow our own path and ignore the rules and guidelines that God has given us.

What is the Church's solution to the problems we face within the home and society?

It is true that we are living in a difficult time with serious problems within the family. But what can the church do about it? Does the church have anything better to offer than society at large, or is the church doomed to take part in the social merry-go-round and sanction a mother's overwhelming double duty of working a job and caring for the home and family? Is this God's calling for the church in solving the burden on home and family? As Christians, we must remember that we should first seek God's kingdom and not build a future on this earth. Like faithful Abraham, we are strangers and aliens on this earth, and we look forward to the city of God. This earthly life is a preparation for the coming, eternal life in God's kingdom.

Ellen White points out the very important duty that parents have to carry out with regard to their children:

> It is the privilege of parents to take their children with them to the gates of the city of God, saying, "I have tried to instruct my children to love the Lord, to do His will, and to glorify Him." To such the gate will be thrown open, and parents and children will enter in. But all cannot enter. Some are left outside with their children, whose characters have not been transformed by submission to the will of God. A hand is raised, and the words are spoken, "You have neglected home duties. You have failed to do the work that would have fitted the soul for a home in heaven. You cannot enter." The gates are closed to the children because they have not learned to do the will of

God, and to parents because they have neglected the responsibilities resting upon them.

Light has been shining from the Word of God and the testimonies of His Spirit so that none need err in regard to their duty. God requires parents to bring up their children to know Him and to respect His claims; they are to train their little ones, as the younger members of the Lord's family, to have beautiful characters and lovely tempers, that they may be fitted to shine in the heavenly courts. By neglecting their duty and indulging their children in wrong, parents close to them the gates of the city of God. These facts must be pressed home upon parents; they must arouse and take up their long-neglected work.[37]

Taking this crucial counsel seriously, would parents ever decide to take their children to a nursery or daycare and entrust the majority of the care and education of their children to others?

The quotation says: "Light has been shining from the Word of God." It is clear that parents must faithfully raise their children in the ways of the Lord and take responsibility for their children's care and the care of their home. Several Bible verses, including Genesis 18:18, 19; Deuteronomy 4:10; 6:4-7; 11:18, 19; 32:46; Psalm 78:5-7; and 1 Timothy 3:4, 5, clearly teach this responsibility.

Hebrew parents were expected to educate their children faithfully, an assignment that they could not lose sight of for a moment. They had to teach and guide their offspring in the ways of the Lord God and constantly talk about it at home and on the road, when lying down and standing up. That says enough. It points to unwavering duty! God's mission is clear: a completely

---
[37] E. G. White, *Child Guidance*, p. 13.

dedicated, uninterrupted education, a full-time duty that applies to parents of all times—including the present—because God is unchangeable.

Hebrew parents were expected to educate their children faithfully, an assignment that they could not lose sight of for a moment

In light of the Scriptural teaching on this subject, can a mother, who carries the largest part of the responsibilities of caring for her children, ever combine her all-encompassing responsibility with a full-time job? Many inspired statements point to the great importance of parents' careful and conscientious fulfilling of their responsibilities in the family, which nothing should ever disrupt.

It is in the home that the education of the child is to begin. Here is his first school. Here, with his parents as instructors, he is to learn the lessons that are to guide him throughout life—lessons of respect, obedience, reverence, self-control. The educational influences of the home are a decided power for good or for evil. They are in many respects silent and gradual, but if exerted on the right side, they become a far-reaching power for truth and righteousness. If the child is not instructed aright here, Satan will educate him through agencies of his choosing. How important, then, is the school in the home!

Upon all parents there rests the obligation of giving physical, mental, and spiritual instruction. It should be the object of every parent to secure to his child a well-balanced, symmetrical character. This is a work of no small magnitude and importance—a work requiring earnest thought and prayer no less than patient, persevering effort. A right foundation must be laid, a framework, strong and firm, erected; and then day by day the work of building, polishing, perfecting, must go forward.[38]

All parents have the obligation of guiding their children physically and spiritually.

Parents, remember that your home is a training school, in which your children are to be prepared for the home above. Deny them anything rather than the education that they should receive in their earliest years....

Let not home education be regarded as a secondary matter. It occupies the first place in all true education. Fathers and mothers have entrusted to them the molding of their children's minds....

Parents, will you remember that the education of your children from their earliest years is committed to you as a sacred trust? These young trees are to be tenderly trained, that they may be transplanted to the garden of the Lord. Home education is not by any means to be neglected. Those who neglect it neglect a religious duty.

---
[38] E. G. White, *Child Guidance*, p. 17.

> God commanded the Hebrews to teach their children His requirements, and to make them acquainted with all His dealings with their people. The home and the school were one. In the place of stranger lips, the loving hearts of the father and mother were to give instruction to their children....
>
> Many who profess to be followers of Christ are sadly neglectful of home duties; they do not perceive the sacred importance of the trust which God has placed in their hands, to so mold the characters of their children that they will have the moral stamina to resist the many temptations that ensnare the feet of youth....
>
> If parents would feel that they are never released from their burden of educating and training their children for God, if they would do their work in faith, co-operating with God by earnest prayer and work, they would be successful in bringing their children to the Saviour.[39]

These unambiguous words are God's fitting answer to the crisis in families of raising and caring for children. This is the very solution the church has to offer our disrupted society, now that much evil and misery comes when parents habitually neglect their family responsibilities and the care of the children is displaced by a job or other professional activities.

In the book *The Adventist Home*, we also read some important statements that have to do with this subject and that are definitely worth considering:

> One great reason why there is so much evil in the world today is that parents occupy their minds with other things than that which is all-important—how to adapt themselves to the work of patiently and kindly teaching their children the way of the Lord. If the curtain could be drawn aside, we should see that

---

[39] Ellen G. White, *Child Guidance*, pp. 17–19, 22.

many, many children who have gone astray have been lost to good influences through this neglect. Parents, can you afford to have it so in your experience? You should have no work so important that it will prevent you from giving to your children all the time that is necessary to make them understand what it means to obey and trust the Lord fully....

The mother must ever stand pre-eminent in this work of training the children; while grave and important duties rest upon the father, the mother, by almost constant association with her children, especially during their tender years, must always be their special instructor and companion.

Parents should be much at home. By precept and example they should teach their children the love and the fear of God; teach them to be intelligent, social, affectionate; to cultivate habits of industry, economy, and self-denial. By giving their children love, sympathy, and encouragement at home, parents may provide for them a safe and welcome retreat from many of the world's temptations.

Parents, you carry responsibilities that no one can bear for you. As long as you live, you are accountable to God to keep His way....

How sad it is that many parents have cast off their God-given responsibility to their children, and are willing that strangers should bear it for them!

No work can equal that of the Christian mother. She takes up her work with a sense of what it is to bring up her children in the nurture and admonition of the Lord.

The king upon his throne has no higher work than has the mother. The mother is queen of her household. She has in her power the molding of her children's characters, that they may be fitted for the higher, immortal life. An angel could not ask for a higher mission; for in doing this work she is doing service for God. Let her only realize the high character of her task, and it will inspire her with courage.

He [God] sees that with proper training the child will become a power for good in the world.... Parents should allow nothing to come between them and the obligation they owe to their children.

Notwithstanding boasted advancement that has been made in educational methods, the training of children at the present day is sadly defective. It is the home training that is neglected. Parents, and especially mothers, do not realize their responsibility. They have neither the patience to instruct nor the wisdom to control the little ones entrusted to their keeping.

It is too true that mothers are not standing at their post of duty, faithful to their motherhood. God requires of us nothing that we cannot in His strength perform, nothing that is not for our own good and the good of our children.[40]

---

[40] E. G. White, *The Adventist Home*, pp. 183–185, 187, 204, 231, 264, 265.

Mothers should remember that their high calling has tremendous, far-reaching consequences. They should recognize that their influence in training their children is more decisive and powerful than the minister in the pulpit or even the king upon his throne:

The mother's daily influence upon her children is preparing them for everlasting life or eternal death. She exercises in her home a power more decisive than the minister in the desk, or even the king upon his throne.[41]

God requires parents to raise their children in the fear of the Lord and to not neglect the responsibilities that rest upon them. If faithfully and conscientiously performed, there will be intense and immeasurable pleasure on the day of the Lord when they are welcomed, together with their children, into the gates of the city of God.

---

[41] E. G. White, *Reflecting Christ*, June 30, p. 195.

The mission of the mother is not to build a career that is respected by society. Her high, unparalleled, royal calling is with her children. She must have her hands free to be present for her children and to faithfully fulfill her responsibilities in caring for the family. It is in fulfillment of her God-given role that she will be saved.

Many problems in society and in the church will be resolved when a mother meets God's standard, faithfully raising her children.

Mothers, shall our precious time be worse than wasted in work and hurry ... while but a limited time is improved in educating and disciplining our children? Our hands are on the cradle that rocks the world. Shall our children become what they may be, and what God would have them be? Shall we meet God's standard, revealed to us in his word, or shall our efforts be employed to meet the world's standard?[42]

God has given the mother, in the education of her children, a responsibility paramount to everything else.[43]

All the tact and cultivated skill of the mother will be called into requisition if she rules with God-fearing wisdom. She will not turn her children over to hired help, or leave them to obtain a street education.[44]

Next to God, the mother's power for good is the strongest known on earth.[45]

The church will bless her because she has educated and developed talent which will be of the highest value. She gives to the church, men and women who

---

[42] E. G. White, *Good Health*, July 1, 1880, p. 207.
[43] E. G. White, *Good Health*, June 1, 1880, p. 174.
[44] E. G. White, *Good Health*, July 1, 1880, p. 207.
[45] E. G. White, *Good Health*, March 1, 1880, p. 77.

will not flinch from duty however taxing. If Christian mothers had always done their work with fidelity, there would not now be so many church trials on account of disorderly members. Mothers are forming the characters which compose the church of God. When I see a church in trial, its members self-willed, heady, high-minded, self-sufficient, not subject to the voice of the church, I am led to fear that their mothers were unfaithful in their early training.[46]

If religion reigns in the home, it will be brought into the church. The parents who do their work for God are a power for good. As they restrain and encourage their children, bringing them up in the nurture and admonition of the Lord, they bless the neighborhood in which they live. And the church is strengthened by their faithful work.[47]

God calls upon the church and parents in raising children to comply with His standard and not the world's. The precious time allotted for the fundamental education of our dear children for eternity should not be wasted on all kinds of other activities and work. Since the heavy responsibility of raising children that is entrusted to parents has such enormous influence in determining this life and the life to come, it requires the parents' full attention. The sacred role of the mother must, therefore, prevail in everything and occupy the first place, and it must not be obstructed by anything or anyone.

It is certainly praiseworthy that three full times the voice of the World Church has rejected the ordination of women to the fulfilling of the full-time leadership and authoritative ministry of the pastor. It should be apparent that it is not possible for a woman and mother to be

---
[46] E. G. White, *Good Health*, April 1, 1880, p. 109.
[47] E. G. White, *Child Guidance*, p. 550.

present on two principal, crucial fronts which equally require full attention, responsibility, and energy: the church and the family. Both are sacred, and each in itself requires a full commitment of time and effort, leaving no room for anything else. We read:

> Let the young man who has entered the ministry look his calling fairly in the face, and determine to devote his time, his strength, his influence, to the work, well aware of the conditions under which he serves the Redeemer.[48]
>
> They [the ministers] give their entire time, thought, and effort to the service of the Master....[49]
>
> Overburdened, a minister is often so hurried that he scarcely finds time to examine himself, whether he be in the faith.[50]

In light of these statements, where is there time for a woman and mother who has been ordained as a minister to devote to the upbringing of her children?

Some say that exercising the right to ordain women is a principle of conscience. It may very well be true that a conscientious ordained woman and mother would inevitably have a torn conscience, at times, in not being able to adequately perform her full-time duties of caring for her family while carrying the responsibilities of full-time ministry as a pastor. She would have to be satisfied with less, either from one responsibility or the other or from both. It is understandable that she would be troubled as a serious, dutiful woman and mother. She would certainly be tormented by the urgent question of how she can justify her choice before God.

---

[48] E. G. White, *Gospel Workers*, p. 104.
[49] E. G. White, *Gospel Workers*, p. 449.
[50] E. G. White, *Evangelism*, p. 91.

Only those who deny both the high calling of full-time motherhood and the full-time ministry of the pastorate can think that they can do both well.

A woman and mother is primarily called to her role in the family, educating her children. She must not allow this extensive sacred duty to be supplanted by another many-faceted full-time job, for this causes God displeasure:

> The mother's work is given her of God, to bring up her children in the nurture and admonition of the Lord.... The mother must engrave upon the tablet of the heart lessons as enduring as eternity; and she will surely meet the displeasure of the Lord if she neglects this sacred work or allows anything to interfere with it. . . . The Christian mother has her God-appointed work, which she will not neglect if she is closely connected with God and imbued with His Spirit.[51]

---
[51] E. G. White, *The Adventist Home*, pp. 233, 234.

The mother's mission in her home is paramount to everything else. If she is faithful to her duties as a mother, she will be listed as one of the greatest missionaries in the world.

> The husband in the open missionary field may receive the honors of men, while the home toiler may receive no earthly credit for her labor. But if she works for the best interest of her family, seeking to fashion their characters after the divine Model, the recording angel writes her name as one of the greatest missionaries in the world. God does not see things as man's finite vision views them most.[52]

Is it appropriate for God's church to encourage women to combine the duties of motherhood with a heavy, responsible task in the church when actual practice has shown that the time and attention for performing the home duties will often be neglected, to some degree, and have subtle, far-reaching consequences in the development of their children? Or should women neglect their responsibilities as mothers to allow them time to fulfill an ecclesiastical office?

Was God's church not appointed by God to set a good example in society, especially regarding the thorough education of children? Should children not be properly raised for eternity? Should this, as befits good Christians, not receive all possible attention? It surely requires undivided priority.

The responsibilities of motherhood are undoubtedly important enough for the mother to resolutely reject any other responsible task that leads to divided attention. No one need be ignorant of the unpleasant consequences of neglected motherhood. Studies have shown that working mothers can have disastrous effects on the

---

[52] E. G. White, *The Adventist Home*, p. 235.

psychological health of their children. The guidelines from God's Word, the testimony of the Spirit of Prophecy, and the findings of research point to the great importance of motherhood and indicate unambiguously that, when mothers do not properly fulfill their home duties, their children are disadvantaged for their entire lives.

God will, without the slightest doubt, hold us to account regarding whether we have faithfully fulfilled our duties according to His revealed will. It is crystal clear that God's sacred mission for mothers, of raising children in the ways of the Lord, is a solemn duty demanding much prayer, patience, wisdom, attention, and dedication. It is a task that requires unremitting, persevering effort. This sacred, crucial duty is greatly ignored and underestimated, and certainly so if we think that we can combine this duty with a proportionately large and extensive responsibility of the office of leadership in the church, a sacred function that also demands full commitment, dedication, attention, and effort. Combining these two tasks is not effectively possible in practice, for it will irrevocably be at the expense of either one or the other or of both. God will certainly not accept half-hearted work, not in caring for the family and the upbringing of children and not in the pastoral and evangelizing tasks of His church. God requires full commitment, both in the family and in the church. God will not settle for anything less.

For women, there are many other, less burdensome opportunities to work in the church, leaving time and opportunity for the faithful fulfillment of their domestic duties.

Those who promote the ordination of women in the ministry bypass the high calling of church and parents to bring up children diligently and undivided for God. The church has, in accordance with God's will, the priority of conscientiously raising children. In fact, it is of paramount importance under its charter.

Nothing is of greater importance than the education of our children and young people. The church should arouse and manifest a deep interest in this work; for now as never before, Satan and his host are determined to enlist the youth under the black banner that leads to ruin and death.

God has appointed the church as a watchman, to have a jealous care over the youth and children, and as a sentinel to see the approach of the enemy and give warning of danger.

If ever we are to work in earnest, it is now. The enemy is pressing in on all sides, like a flood. Only the power of God can save our children from being swept away by the tide of evil. The responsibility resting upon parents, teachers, and church members, to do their part in co-operation with God, is greater than words can express.[53]

---
[53] E. G. White, *Counsels to Parents, Teachers and Students*, pp. 165, 166.

The church is not called to override the mother's parenting obligation in the family by ordaining her to another notable and demanding task in the church. On the contrary, the church must take its stand for the great importance of the careful upbringing of children.

As a watchman appointed by God, the church, with sacred motivation and jealous care, must see to it that children are not spiritually deformed but that they receive a proper education due them to save them from death and destruction.

God has most certainly not appointed the church to violate the mother's all-important responsibilities, which affect the eternal preservation of her children. God in no wise calls a mother to share the heavy, full-time burden of motherhood with yet another full-time, authoritative position of leadership in the church.

Consider Ellen White's message to a mother who thought that the Lord would have her engage in ministerial work—a great and holy work with religious duties—attending meetings, giving Bible readings, and presenting messages to others. This is undoubtedly important work, and some mothers may feel that God has called them to the ministry, but consider Ellen White's clear words:

> The Lord has a work for you to do; it is not a public work, but a very important one, a work in your own home, to be true to your position as a wife and mother. No other can do this, your work. The Spirit and the Word of God agree. Remembering this, let us read the words of inspiration from Jesus Christ through Paul to Titus. He is charged to speak "the things which become sound doctrine: ... The aged women likewise ... that they may teach the young women to be sober, to love their husbands, to love their children,

to be discreet, chaste, keepers at home, good, obedient to their own husbands, that the Word of God be not blasphemed."[54] (Titus 2:1-5.) With this Scripture before you, I ask, For what are you spending your time in Battle Creek? Has God called you to neglect your home? No, no.

My sister, the Lord has shown me that you are mistaking your duty. Your husband needs you; your children need their mother. You have stepped out of the path where Jesus leads the way. He is saying to you, "Follow me," and He will lead you in your own home duties, which are now sadly neglected. The voice of the Lord has not bidden you to separate your interests from that of your husband and children. Your first duty is in the home. The Spirit of the Lord has not given you a work or qualified you to do a work, that is contrary to His own Word....

You have a great work, a sacred, holy calling to exemplify the Christian graces as a faithful wife and mother; to be lovable, patient, kind, yet firm in your home life, to learn right methods and acquire tact for the training of your own little ones, that they may keep the way of the Lord. As a humble child of God, learn in the school of Christ, seek constantly to improve your powers to do the most perfect, thorough work at home, both by precept and example.

---

[54] Regarding the phrase, "keepers at home," we read: "... in Greek *oikoergos*, from *oikos*, 'home' and *ergon*, 'work.' Both parts should be properly emphasized. Firstly, the young woman must understand that her field of work is at home and not in public life.... In the second place, the emphasis is on 'work': she must not spend her time at home in idleness but to do the work that has to be done so that her family is not neglected.... The 'home' is not just the house, but often means the family in Scripture. The intention is therefore that the young women must feel their responsibility for all the work that has to be done at home, not just caring for outward things (clothing, etc.) but also the spiritual care of the children by praying with them and pointing them to the Lord Jesus" (W. J. Ouweneel, *De Brief van Paulus aan Titus* [Uit het Woord der Waarheid, Winschoten], p. 122, translated from Dutch).

In this work you will have the help of the Lord; but if you ignore your duty as a wife and mother, and hold out your hands for the Lord to put another class of work in them, be sure that He will not contradict Himself; He points you to the duty you have to do at home. If you have the idea that some work greater and holier than this has been entrusted to you, you are under a deception. In neglecting your husband and children for what you suppose to be religious duties, either to attend meetings or to work for others, to give Bible readings or to have messages for others, you are going directly contrary to the words of inspiration in the instruction of Paul to Titus. The religion of Christ never leads a wife and mother to do as you have done....

The Saviour discerns a value and dignity in every soul, because of the image of God which it bears. He died that your children might have the gift of eternal life. He looks upon them with divine compassion. Their souls may be saved unto eternal life, and they are just as precious as the souls of others. The Lord has not called you to neglect your home and your husband and children. He never works in this way; and He never will. You have before your own door a little plot of ground to care for, and God will hold you responsible for this work which He has left in your hands....

If you are one of those who are the light of the world, that light is to shine in your home.... Never for a moment suppose that God has given you a work that will necessitate a separation from your precious little flock. Do not leave them to become demoralized by improper associations and to harden their hearts against their mother. This is letting your light shine in a wrong way altogether; you are making it more

> difficult for your children to become what God would have them and win heaven at last. God cares for them, and so must you if you claim to be His child....
>
> Your husband has rights; your children have rights; and these must not be ignored by you. Whether you have one talent or three or five, God has given you your work. Parents are fearfully neglectful of their home duties. They do not meet the Bible standard. But to those who forsake their homes, their companions and children, God will not entrust the work of saving souls, for they have proved unfaithful to their holy vows. They have proved unfaithful to sacred responsibilities. God will not entrust to them eternal riches....
>
> The Christian mother's work begins in the home circle, in making her home what it should be, pleasant to her husband, pleasant to her children. These dear ones are in her hands to educate faithfully....[55]

These words clearly indicate that the Holy Spirit does not call mothers as He does men to work in the gospel ministry. The opposite belief does not meet the Bible standard. The souls of their children are just as precious as the souls of others, and it is the mothers' calling to faithfully work for their salvation. If mothers neglect this calling, God will not entrust to them the work of saving souls. They have proved themselves unfaithful.

Ellen White pointed out that mothers should not be engaged in full-time gospel ministry but, rather, should be faithful missionaries in their own homes:

> God does not call mothers away from home missionary work which will leave their children under the control of influences that are demoralizing and ruinous to the soul. Are not her children in need of missionary labor?

---

[55] E. G. White, Lt. 28, 1890, *Manuscript Releases*, Vol. 8, pp. 433-437.

Are not her children worth earnest and prayerful effort? Shall she neglect home missionary work for a larger field? Let her try her skill in her own home—take up her appointed, God-given work....

Consider yourself as God's appointed missionary, to be the light of your home. Again I say, It is not like the works of God to call the mother away from her husband and from her children to engage in what she considers higher work....

I am pained when I receive letters from mothers who have children inquiring, Shall I leave my children to do missionary work? In the fear and love of God, I say, become a home missionary. Educate yourself in Bible ways and means that you may be a successful worker in your own home, for you see they need to be saved, for they are sinners. Do not forsake your post of duty....[56]

> *The souls of their children are just as precious as the souls of others, and it is the mothers' calling to faithfully work for their salvation*

Now, this does not mean that women are completely excluded from gospel work or pastoral duties. No, certainly not.

Although Ellen White nowhere speaks of women as ordained full-time ministers, it is good to note that she speaks of women pastors, indicating that if they are free, God's Spirit may prepare them to perform pastoral duties. She stated: "It is the accompaniment of the Holy Spirit of God that prepares workers, both men and

---
[56] E. G. White, Ms. 9, 1868, *Manuscript Releases,* Vol. 3, pp. 371, 372.

women, to become pastors to the flock of God." (RH Jan. 15, 1901.)

Women spending part of their time in the service of God, certainly need God's blessing and Ellen White counsels that they should be dedicated by prayer and laying on of hands: "Women who are willing to consecrate some of their time to the service of the Lord should be appointed to visit the sick, look after the young, and minister to the necessities of the poor. They should be set apart to this work by prayer and laying on of hands." (RH July 9, 1895.)

Ellen White is versatile and describes various possible situations. We must not misuse her words or read them out of context. We can understand all of her statements not as contradictory but in harmony and in balance with each other.

Children are different. Little ones need a mother's care, but more grown ups are often less dependent. Some are in need of guidance for a long time, while others are quickly balanced, firm and more independent. The freedom and possibilities of a mother, for part-time gospel work, depends on the circumstances of each family and this must carefully and under prayer be assessed and weighed, because necessary childcare always takes precedence.

Without being ordained, a woman who has no children or no young children can do gospel work. Especially a pastor's wife can help her husband well. We read:

> And if the Lord gives the wife, as well as the husband, the burden of labor, and if she devotes her time and her strength to visiting from family to family, opening the Scriptures to them, although the hands of ordination have not been laid upon

her, she is accomplishing a work that is in the line of ministry.... If a woman puts her housework in the hands of a faithful, prudent helper, and leaves her children in good care, while she engages in the work, the conference should have wisdom to understand the justice of her receiving wages.... Letters have come to me from several, asking my advice upon the question, Should ministers' wives adopt infant children? Would I advise them to do this kind of work? To some who were regarding this matter favorably, I answered, No; God would have you help your husband in his work. The Lord has not given you children of your own; His wisdom is not to be questioned. He knows what is best. Consecrate your powers to God as a Christian worker. You can help your husband in many ways. You can support him in his work by working for him, by keeping your intellect improved. By using the ability God has given you, you can be a home-keeper. And more than this, you can help to give the message.... But the wives of our ministers, who can themselves act a part in the work of educating others, should in the love of God be co-laborers with Christ. Let them not voluntarily tie their hands by the care of an infant.[57]

We may understand that if there are small children, mothers must faithfully fulfill their duty by being a missionary at home. If there are no children, the advice is that a minister's wife should not adopt an infant but help her husband. And if there are grown up children, then a minister's wife can possibly leave them in good care of a faithful, prudent helper to be free to stand next to her husband in the gospel ministry. We read:

---
[57] E. G. White, *Manuscript Releases*, vol. 5, pp. 323–327.

"The woman, if she is devoted and free to do so, can reach as much as he does by standing next to her husband."[58]

Ellen White makes clear that in a family with children, the parental-motherhood duties do not very well combine and harmonize with being engaged in Gospel missionary work. There is division – hands and hearts are not free. Note what she explains:

"In sending missionaries to distant countries, those men should be selected who know how to economize, who have not large families, and who, realizing the shortness of time and the great work to be accomplished, will not fill their hands and houses with children, but will keep themselves as free as possible from everything that will divert their minds from their one great work. The wife, if devoted, and left free to do so, can, by standing by the side of her husband, accomplish as much as he. God has blessed woman with talents to be used to his glory in bringing many sons and daughters to God; but many who might be efficient laborers are kept at home to care for their little ones. We want missionaries who are missionaries in the fullest sense of the word... Many who have families go out to labor, but they do not give themselves entirely to the work. Their minds are divided. Wife and children draw them from their labor, and often keep them out of fields that they might enter were it not that they think they must be near their home. Let missionaries be missionaries; let them leave their own and their wives' hands and hearts free, taking their homes with them where they go, and great good will be accomplished."[59]

---
[58] E. G. White, *Gospel Workers*, p. 459.
[59] *Review and Herald*, December 8, 1885, para. 8

Since God has not called mothers with children to engage in missionary work outside their homes, how then can some leaders within the church plead for their ordination? Those who think that women should be ordained to the same ministry as men are part of the sleeping church, not realizing the importance of the duties of motherhood in training and educating their children.

The church is asleep and does not realize the magnitude of this matter of educating the children and youth.[60]

To the mother and father the right training of their children is the most important work of their life.[61]

Note how extremely important the work of bringing up the children in the way of the Lord really is. It is the greatest work ever committed to mortals! Those who strive to ordain women to a heavy, full-time office of responsibility in the church are certainly asleep. They tragically underestimate the interference that such a full-time job definitely will have on the God-given greatest work of faithfully performing the duties of motherhood. They will certainly be negatively affected, and what will be the result? Are you willing to run the risk of your children one day cursing you because their education has not been your priority?

Fathers and mothers, how stands your record? Have you been faithful to your trust? ... Mothers, have you neglected your God-given work—the greatest work ever committed to mortals? Have you refused to bear your God-given responsibilities? In the time of trouble just before us, when the judgments of God

---
[60] E. G. White, *Child Guidance*, p. 332.
[61] E. G. White, *Child Guidance*, p. 556.

fall upon the impure and unholy, will your children curse you because of your indulgence?[62]

Time is short, and now more than ever we should do our utmost to train and educate our dear children in faith that they may be saved in God's Kingdom. It is not too late to bring about a reformation in the home in harmony with God's plan. The reward for our faithful efforts will be immense.

> *Time is short, and now more than ever we should do our utmost to train and educate our dear children in faith that they may be saved in God's Kingdom*

Coming events are casting their shadows upon our pathway. Fathers, mothers, I appeal to you to make most earnest efforts now for your children. Give them daily religious instruction. Teach them to love God and to be true to the principles of right. With lofty, earnest faith, directed by the divine influence of the Holy Spirit, work, work now. Do not put it off one day, one hour.[63]

Suppose you should get to heaven and none of your children be there. How could you say to God, "Here am I, Lord, and the children which Thou hast given me"? Heaven marks the neglect of parents. It is recorded in the books of heaven.[64]

Parents, humble your hearts before God. Begin a thorough work with your children. Plead with the Lord to forgive your disregard of His Word in neglecting to train your children in the way they should go. Ask for light and guidance, for a tender conscience, and for

---

[62] E. G. White, *Child Guidance*, p. 556.
[63] E. G. White, *Child Guidance*, p. 557.
[64] E. G. White, *Child Guidance*, p. 561.

clear discernment that you may see your mistakes and failures. God will hear such prayers from a humble and contrite heart.

If you have failed in your duty to your families, confess your sins before God. Gather your children about you and acknowledge your neglect. Tell them that you desire to bring about a reformation in the home, and ask them to help you to make the home what it ought to be. Read to them the directions found in the Word of God. Pray with them; and ask God to spare their lives, and to help them to prepare for a home in His kingdom.[65]

Never be satisfied to have your children grow up apart from Christ. Never feel at ease while they are cold and indifferent. Cry to God day and night. Pray and work for the salvation of the souls of your children.[66]

It will pay in the end for mothers to make the formation of the characters of their children their first and highest consideration, that the thorns may not take root and yield an abundant harvest.

Oh, that parents would look prayerfully and carefully after their children's eternal welfare! Let them ask themselves, Have we been careless? Have we neglected this solemn work? Have we allowed our children to become the sport of Satan's temptations? Have we not a solemn account to settle with God because we have permitted our children to use their talents, their time and influence, in working against the truth, against Christ? Have we not neglected our duty as parents and increased the number of the subjects of Satan's kingdom?[67]

When the judgment shall sit, and the books

---
[65] E. G. White, *Child Guidance*, p. 557.
[66] E. G. White, *Child Guidance*, p. 558.
[67] E. G. White, *Child Guidance*, p. 563.

shall be opened; when the "well done" of the great Judge is pronounced, and the crown of immortal glory is placed upon the brow of the victor, many will raise their crowns in sight of the assembled universe and, pointing to their mother, say, "She made me all I am through the grace of God. Her instruction, her prayers, have been blessed to my eternal salvation."[68]

The more we dwell on the influence, scope, and effect of the faithful performance of the duties of motherhood, the more we will come to realize that, in the light of eternity, a mother can not allow herself to be distracted from her high vocation. Nothing should intervene that will hinder a careful, consecrated fulfillment of a mother's duties.

We ought to be very grateful that God has faithfully guided His church in this important and serious matter, in accordance with His revealed requirements, precepts, and will.

The pioneers of the SDA church stood firmly upon the Biblical platform. They simply believed what the Bible says.

Daniel T. Bourdeau, a prominent SDA pioneer, evangelist and missionary, referring to 1 Tim. 2:9-13, wrote: "Here again we have the idea of subjection. Paul does not suffer a woman to teach, or to usurp authority over the man; and we do not learn from the Scriptures that women were ever ordained (as) apostles, evangelists or elders; neither do we believe that they should teach as such. Yet they may act an important part in speaking the truth to others." (RH, December 2, 1862, p. 6).

In the early days of the SDA church, there was no divison about this issue; the testimony of the Scriptures was decisive and the church was well founded.

---

[68] E. G. White, *Child Guidance*, p. 564.

Although it is certainly not God's plan and purpose that a mother with young children should work, it is regrettable that sometimes circumstances exist in which a mother is forced to work in order to survive with her children.

This is, however, not according to biblical precept. The Bible clearly associates the calling of the mother with her children and not with public work or with the high authoritative office of pastoral leadership within the church (1 Tim. 2:15).

The Greek word that is used in this verse, *teknogonia*, which means "giving birth to children," also includes, by implication, the duties of motherhood.[69]

J. A. Bengel commented on this verse: "The woman's office is here described, in the contrast with the duty of teaching and governing: *bringing forth and training children.*"[70]

The Aramaic translation of 1 Timothy 2:15, as rendered in the *Passion Translation*, reads:

> Yet a woman shall live in restored dignity by means of her children, receiving the blessing that comes from raising them as consecrated children nurtured in faith and love, walking in wisdom.

In the *Peshitta* Bible, the authorized Bible of the Church of the East, this verse reads:

> Nevertheless, if her posterity continue in faith and have holiness and charity, she will live through them. (Lamsa)

Thus, the Bible clearly indicates that women are called to fulfill the duty of raising and educating their children in the faith. That is the way to life for them and their children.

---

[69] W. E. Vine, *Expository Dictionary of New Testament Words*, p. 180; Ethelbert W. Bullinger, *A Critical Lexicon and Concordance to the English and Greek New Testament*, p. 150; James Strong, *The Exhaustive Concordance of the Bible*, p. 71.

[70] John Albert Bengel, *Gnomon of the New Testament*, vol. 2, p. 515.

The apostle Paul reminds Timothy of the unfeigned faith that lived first in his grandmother Lois and also in his mother Eunice. Both had faithfully transferred their faith to their offspring (2 Tim. 1:5). Further on Paul then wrote:

> But continue thou in the things which thou hast learned and hast been assured of, knowing of whom thou hast learned them; and that from a child thou hast known the holy scriptures, which are able to make thee wise unto salvation through faith which is in Christ Jesus. (2 Tim. 3:14, 15)

It is undisputedly God's intention that the task of life for women and mothers is that they transfer the faith to their children so that they will be saved for God's kingdom.

It is undisputedly God's intention that the task of life for women and mothers is that they transfer the faith to their children so that they will be saved for God's kingdom

Those who advocate and proclaim the ordination of women thwart God's plan. They must come to realize that they are burdening mothers, in addition to what research has identified as the two and half full-time jobs of motherhood, with another heavy full-time job in the church.

This is irresponsible and unacceptable for the physical and emotional health of women, and it piles on them discriminately when men usually only perform one full-time job. After all, the general rule in practice is that men's share of the responsibilities of the home is relatively small because the mother does almost everything for the children.

Those who, nevertheless, continue to support women's ordination may certainly know that with this abusive attitude they are more in harmony with the world and completely out of step with the guidelines of the revealed Word of God and with the instructions of the Spirit of Prophecy.

Society itself has many critical voices raising concern over the many negative consequences of neglected motherhood. Knowing about these consequences should encourage Christians to open-mindedly re-consider the precious precepts that God has given us for the family and for the upbringing of our children.

We must remember, however, that in the Bible, in the calling of women, no exception is made for those who are not married or do not have children, as if for them different rules would apply. No, there is no indication for that. The Bible says that the desire of a woman goes out to her husband and, thus, she may meet a suitable partner later in life and possibly have a child when she is older than usual.[71]

Another important point, which certainly makes one think, is that many young people often show little interest in religion. Many leave the church as soon as they have become independent. Some think that we need to lower the membership threshold for the church and adjust church services by introducing popular messages and music with a beat, but this has not proven effective in keeping young people in the church. The purpose of the church service is to honor God, not to please young people. No, that is not what a servant of God will do. The apostle Paul testifies: "If I were still trying to please men, I would not be a servant of Christ."[72] If we adapt our church services

---
[71] Gen. 3:16.
[72] Gal. 1:10, Berean Study Bible.

to satisfy young people and keep them in the church, we are certainly not doing well, and our efforts will ultimately not be able to stand for eternity. No, that is not the solution. The problem is clearly on a different level. We need to focus our attention and energy, as the main focus of our lives, on something else. We read:

> Unless parents shall make it the first business of their lives to guide their children's feet into the path of righteousness from their earliest years, the wrong path will be chosen before the right.[73]

This is the real problem. If parents would diligently guide and educate their young children in the ways of the Lord, then they would not so easily choose a wrong path. Unfortunately, the impact of this important work has not been sufficiently realized. The promise, however, is that watchful, prayerful, persevering efforts will be successful:

> I tremble especially for mothers, as I see them so blind, and feeling so little the responsibilities that devolve upon a mother.[74]
>
> Watch and pray. You will have a battle, parents, to dispossess your child of the Satanic spirit; but you will succeed if you are persevering.[75]
>
> There has been altogether too little attention paid to our children and youth, and they have failed to develop as they should in the Christian life.... The Lord is not glorified when the children are neglected and passed by.... They need painstaking, prayerful, careful labor.[76]

When you stand before the great white throne, then

---
[73] E. G. White, *Child Guidance*, p. 489.
[74] E. G. White, *Child Guidance*, p. 289.
[75] E. G. White, *Review and Herald*, April 14, 1885, p. 225.
[76] E. G. White, *Child Guidance*, p. 488.

your work will appear as it is.... To many parents the Judge will say in that day, "You had My Word, plainly setting forth your duty. Why have you not obeyed its teachings? Knew ye not that it was the voice of God? Did I not bid you search the Scriptures, that you might not go astray? ..."[77]

Heaven is worth everything to us. We must not run any risk in this matter. We must take no venture here....

It is the joy of seeing that your efforts, mothers, are rewarded. Here are your children; the crown of life is upon their heads, and the angels of God immortalize the names of the mothers whose efforts have won their children to Jesus Christ.[78]

May God's Spirit enlighten our minds and equip us with clear discernment that we may understand God's intentions and see that it is His revealed will that the upbringing of children is the highest priority of a mother, a duty that requires dedicated, disciplined care and attention. They must recognize that guiding their children is a mission of eternal interest, which certainly cannot be repressed or neglected in any sense by a job outside the home or by transferring their responsibility to others.

May we be faithful and devoted in obediently fulfilling our duties and the responsibilities that God requires of us, and may we not allow ourselves to be distracted and carried away by popular practices that are not in harmony with God's purpose. Only then can we trust that, through God's grace, we will enter the gates of the New Jerusalem together with our children.

J. Voerman, Geesbrug, April 2018.
www.lampofgold.com

---

[77] E. G. White, *Child Guidance*, p. 568, 569.
[78] E. G. White, *Child Guidance*, p. 567, 568.

TEACH Services, Inc.
P U B L I S H I N G

We invite you to view the complete
selection of titles we publish at:
www.TEACHServices.com

We encourage you to write us
with your thoughts about this,
or any other book we publish at:
info@TEACHServices.com

TEACH Services' titles may be purchased in
bulk quantities for educational, fund-raising,
business, or promotional use.
bulksales@TEACHServices.com

Finally, if you are interested in seeing
your own book in print, please contact us at:
publishing@TEACHServices.com
We are happy to review your manuscript at no charge.

www.ingramcontent.com/pod-product-compliance
Ingram Content Group UK Ltd.
Pitfield, Milton Keynes, MK11 3LW, UK
UKHW021957220326
11408UKWH00003B/357